COGNITIVE THERAPY GUIDE

Treatment Solutions For Brain Fog And Mental Fatigue

Regain Cognitive Clarity With Therapeutic Interventions Targeting Brain Fog And Mental Fatigue

DR. BRIDGET PROMISE

Table of Contents

CHAPTER ONE

Introduction

Amidst the fast-paced nature of contemporary society, the pursuit of cognitive clarity has assumed unprecedented importance.

In the face of day-to-day obstacles, encompassing both personal and professional spheres, the capacity for lucid thought, sound decision-making, and cognitive sharpness is of the utmost importance.

This investigation examines the notion of cognitive clarity, assessing its importance, the challenges it encounters in the shape of mental fatigue and brain confusion, and the therapeutic strategies that can be utilized to improve cognitive performance.

Comprehension Of Cognitive Clarity Therapies

Cognitive clarity is a condition characterized by heightened mental acuity and vigilance, which enables an individual to engage in precise thought processes, information processing, and decision-making.

It comprises a multitude of cognitive processes, such as attention, memory, problem-solving, and decision-making. To attain cognitive clarity, one must possess an unobstructed mind that functions at its highest potential, devoid of any impediments that might hinder cognitive processes.

The condition of cognitive clarity is not a fixed state, but rather a fluid interaction of multiple factors. The state of mental lucidity may be affected by dietary habits, stress levels, sleep quality, and overall psychological health. Optimal levels of these factors result in enhanced cognitive function for individuals, which subsequently contributes to increased productivity and an improved quality of life.

The Effects Of Cognitive Distraction And Fatigue

Brain confusion and mental fatigue, in contrast to cognitive clarity, are antithetical to mental acuity. Brain fog is distinguished by symptoms such as impaired concentration, mental haze, and a lack of clarity.

It may present itself in the form of forgetfulness, perplexity, or a feeling of mental inundation. Conversely, mental fatigue pertains to a condition of exhaustion that has an impact on one's cognitive functioning. Mental fatigue is characterized by diminished concentration, increased difficulty in making decisions, and compromised cognitive function as a whole.

A multitude of factors contribute to the development of cognitive fatigue and fogginess. Certain medical conditions, chronic tension, inadequate sleep, and poor nutrition, as well as sedentary lifestyles, are frequent contributors. Particularly, stress causes the secretion of hormones such as cortisol, which, over time, can impair cognitive function.

Additionally, cognitive abilities are weakened and memory consolidation is disrupted due to insufficient sleep.

Brain lethargy and mental fatigue have repercussions that transcend the subjective experience of the affected individual. Decreased cognitive lucidity can result in decreased productivity, erroneous judgment, and heightened workplace tension in professional environments.

CHAPTER TWO

Exposing Therapeutic Methods

There is a growing trend among individuals to pursue therapeutic methods to improve cognitive lucidity, combat brain confusion, and alleviate mental fatigue. These methodologies include dietary interventions, mindfulness practices, lifestyle modifications, and, in certain instances, medical interventions.

1. Optimising Sleep Patterns: Quality sleep is considered a fundamental cornerstone of cognitive health. It is imperative to

establish consistent sleep patterns and guarantee sufficient sleep to maintain optimal cognitive function. The brain consolidates memories, processes information, and eliminates pollutants while asleep, all of which contribute to the maintenance of peak cognitive function during wakefulness.

2. Strategies for Stress Management: Prolonged stress plays a substantial role in the deterioration of cognitive function. Engaging in stress management practices, including but not limited to yoga, deep breathing exercises, and mindfulness meditation, can facilitate the

regulation of stress hormones and enhance cognitive lucidity. In addition to mitigating the detrimental effects of stress on cognitive function, these practices also promote holistic wellness.

3. Promoting Cognitive Health through Nutrition: An optimally balanced diet that is abundant in vital nutrients is indispensable for optimal cognitive performance. Brain health is significantly supported by nutrients including antioxidants, vitamins, minerals, omega-3 fatty acids, and antioxidants. Fatty fish, leafy greens, legumes, and whole grains are examples of foods that

promote cognitive lucidity and provide protection against cognitive decline.

4. Consistent engagement in physical activity has been associated with enhanced cognitive function and a diminished likelihood of experiencing cognitive decline. Enhanced cognitive acuity is a result of the increased blood flow to the brain, stimulation of neurotransmitter release, and promotion of new neuronal growth that all result from regular aerobic exercise.

5. Cognitive Training and Brain Games: Participating in cognitive training exercises, puzzles, and games that present cognitive challenges can aid in the maintenance and enhancement of cognitive function. A multitude of cognitive processes are stimulated by these activities, such as attention, memory, and problem-solving abilities.

6. Nootropic supplements comprise nootropics, which are substances that have the potential to enhance motivation, creativity, and cognitive function. Even though research into their efficacy is ongoing, some individuals claim

to have benefited from vitamins, amino acids, and specific botanicals. Nevertheless, it is critical to exercise prudence when utilizing these and to seek guidance from a healthcare expert.

7. Professional Guidance and Cognitive Behavioral Therapy: Seeking the counsel of healthcare professionals, such as psychologists or cognitive behavioral therapists, can prove to be beneficial for individuals encountering persistent cognitive challenges. By addressing thought patterns and behaviors that contribute to cognitive issues, cognitive behavioral therapy

(CBT) can provide practical strategies for improvement.

In summary, cognitive clarity is a fluid condition that is affected by a multitude of elements; therefore, its acquisition necessitates a comprehensive approach to psychological health. Recognizing the consequences of brain confusion and mental fatigue emphasizes the criticality of implementing therapeutic strategies that foster cognitive well-being. By adopting lifestyle adjustments, participating in mindfulness exercises, ensuring adequate nutrition, and consulting professionals when necessary, individuals can proactively strive to attain and sustain cognitive clarity in their day-to-day activities.

Strategies For Cognitive Enhancement Through Diet:

Brain function is significantly influenced by the food that we eat. Specific nutrients have been identified as contributors to cognitive function and brain health. Omega-3 fatty acids, which are abundant in flaxseeds and fatty fish such as salmon, are vital for maintaining the structural integrity of brain cell membranes. A decreased risk of cognitive decline and enhanced cognitive performance have been linked to their usage.

Neuroprotectants, found in an assortment of fruits and vegetables, avert oxidative stress, a factor that may be associated with the deterioration of cognitive function. Antioxidant-rich berries, in particular, have been associated with improved memory and cognitive function.

Furthermore, it is critical to maintain stable blood sugar levels to ensure optimal cognitive function. Complex carbohydrates, including whole grains, supply the brain with a consistent supply of glucose, which serves as its principal energy source. Conversely, maintaining a healthy reduction in refined sugar consumption aids in averting the cognitive impairment that is linked to fluctuations in blood sugar levels.

The inclusion of foods that enhance cognitive function in one's diet not only confers immediate benefits but also functions as a preventative strategy against cognitive decline associated with aging.

CHAPTER THREE

The Effects Of Physical Activity On Mental Clarity:

Engaging in physical activity not only contributes significantly to the maintenance of cardiovascular health but also enhances mental acuity and cognitive performance.

Consistent physical activity has been associated with the secretion of neurotransmitters such as dopamine and serotonin, which serve to modulate mood and enhance cognitive concentration.

Cycling, sprinting, and swimming are examples of aerobic exercises that increase blood flow to the brain, thereby stimulating the development of new blood vessels and neurons. Neurogenesis is an essential process in the preservation of cognitive function and the prevention of cognitive decline associated with aging.

Moreover, it has been demonstrated that exercise decreases inflammation, a factor linked to a variety of cognitive disorders. Brain pathologies such as neurodegenerative diseases and cognitive impairment may result from inflammatory processes that occur within the body. Consistent participation in physical exercise can help individuals reduce inflammation and promote optimal brain function.

The cognitive capabilities that are positively influenced by exercise include but are not limited to memory, attention, and problem-solving skills. Integrating consistent physical activity into one's daily regimen constitutes a comprehensive strategy for enhancing both physical and mental welfare.

Importance Of Sleep Hygiene For Mental Alertness

Sleep quality and quantity are of the utmost importance for cognitive function and mental alertness. Brain functions such as memory consolidation, learning integration, and the elimination of substances that accumulate during the day are performed during sleep.

Prolonged sleep deprivation or substandard sleep quality may lead to cognitive impairments such as compromised memory function, shortened attention span, and diminished problem-solving capabilities. Neurodegenerative disorders have also been associated with an elevated risk of developing chronic sleep deprivation.

The establishment of sound sleep hygiene practices is critical to maximize the quality of sleep. This entails establishing and adhering to a consistent sleep routine, furnishing an environment conducive to rest, and restricting pre-sleep electronic device usage. In addition, minimizing the consumption of stimulants such as caffeine before slumber may enhance the quality of one's sleep.

Ensuring adequate sleep is a fundamental component in the pursuit of cognitive improvement. It facilitates information consolidation and rejuvenation of the brain, thereby guaranteeing optimal cognitive functioning while awake.

Techniques For Stress Reduction And Mindfulness

The relationship between the mind and body significantly influences cognitive function. Chronic stress has been found to have detrimental effects on both mental health and cognitive function. Mindfulness and stress reduction techniques present efficacious approaches for stress management and the enhancement of cognitive lucidity.

Originating in ancient meditation techniques, mindfulness entails directing one's attention to the current moment without evaluative bias. Consistent engagement in mindfulness meditation has been linked to structural modifications in the brain, such as heightened density of gray matter in regions associated with introspection, compassion, and self-awareness.

Yoga, progressive muscle relaxation, and deep breathing are all stress reduction techniques that stimulate the body's relaxation response. These techniques reduce the synthesis of stress hormones, thereby promoting a state of mental tranquility and concentration.

Excessive secretion of cortisol, a hormone that can impair memory and cognitive function, can result from chronic stress. Through the integration of mindfulness and stress reduction practices into their daily routines, people can alleviate the adverse effects of stress on the brain and augment their cognitive capacities as a whole.

In conclusion, cognitive enhancement can be substantially advanced through the implementation of a holistic approach that incorporates dietary strategies, regular exercise, proper sleep hygiene, and mindfulness practices. In addition to facilitating immediate mental acuity, these lifestyle elements are pivotal in averting age-related cognitive deterioration and fostering enduring brain well-being.

CHAPTER FOUR

Cognitive Exercises And Training Of The Brain

As proactive measures to achieve optimal cognitive function and mental acuity, an increasing number of individuals are turning to cognitive training and brain exercises.

Cognitive training consists of performing tasks that improve memory, stimulate the brain, and increase overall cognitive abilities.

The complexity of these exercises differs, with each exercise focusing on a distinct facet of cognition, including information processing speed, problem-solving abilities, and memory retention.

Like every other muscle in the body, consistent exercise is beneficial for the brain. Participating in cognitive training exercises not only aids in the preservation of cognitive functions but also potentially enhances cognitive reserve—a notion positing that mental stimulation provides a safeguard against cognitive deterioration in old age.

Brain Games and Puzzles: Brain games and puzzles are a well-liked method of cognitive training. It is well-known that logic games, crossword puzzles, and Sudoku stimulate the mind and increase cognitive flexibility. By necessitating critical thinking, strategic problem-solving, and strategic planning, these activities foster neural plasticity—the brain's capacity to restructure itself through the formation of new neural connections.

Memory is an essential component of cognitive functioning, and a multitude of exercises are designed to improve this attribute. Memory recall exercises that require the memorization of lists or sequences, mnemonic devices, and memory recall games have all been shown to be effective methods for enhancing memory retention. The complexity of these exercises can range from simple memorization of purchasing lists to complex memorization of poetry.

Neurofeedback Training: An advanced form of cognitive training, neurofeedback consists of real-time feedback to the individual and the monitoring of brainwave activity. Using this procedure, persons can acquire the ability to regulate and control their EEG patterns, which may have the potential to enhance their attention, focus, and overall cognitive performance. Although this technique is frequently employed in clinical environments, home-based neurofeedback systems are gaining in popularity.

Supplements For Nootropics And Cognitive Enhancement

With the aim of augmenting cognitive function, nootropics have garnered considerable attention as substances that potentially have a beneficial impact. Nootropics, which are alternatively referred to as smart medications or cognitive enhancers, comprise an extensive array of natural and synthetic substances employed by individuals to augment memory, foster creativity, and optimize overall cognitive functioning.

Natural nootropics comprise a variety of substances that are regarded as such on account of their presumed cognitive advantages. Instances include caffeine, which is present in tea and coffee and is recognized for its ability to increase alertness and stimulate the system. Fish oil is a rich source of omega-3 fatty acids, an additional natural nootropic that has been linked to enhanced cognitive function.

Synthetic nootropics, conversely, are substances that have been specifically engineered to augment cognitive functions. A medication used to treat sleep disorders, modafinil, is also recognized for its off-label application as a cognitive enhancer. The racetams, which belong to a category of synthetic compounds, are thought to improve cognitive function and memory.

Nootropics, including herbal supplements like Bacopa monnieri and Ginkgo biloba, are also recognized as cognitive enhancers. For centuries, these botanicals have been utilized in traditional medicine to enhance cognition. It is hypothesized that Ginkgo biloba specifically increases cerebral blood flow, which may have the capacity to enhance memory and cognitive function.

Even though some individuals have reported positive effects from nootropics, the discipline as a whole is still the subject of extensive research. Before incorporating these substances into one's routine, it is prudent to seek guidance from healthcare professionals due to potential variations in their efficacy and safety.

The Impact Of Hydration On Cognitive Performance

The importance of hydration transcends mere physical health; it also exerts a critical influence on cognitive functioning. Cognitive function can be significantly impaired by dehydration, manifesting in changes to mood, concentration, and overall mental acuity.

Due to its high sensitivity to variations in hydration levels, the brain, which is composed primarily of water, requires adequate fluid consumption to ensure optimal cognitive performance.

The impact of dehydration on cognitive function is such that even moderate symptoms can result in impairments. Dehydration has been associated with concentration difficulties, an increased perception of task difficulty, and mood disturbances, according to research. The deterioration of memory and attention that occurs with the progression of dehydration underscores the complex relationship between hydration status and cognitive functions.

Sufficient Hydration for Optimal Cognitive Performance: Achieving optimal hydration necessitates more than mere water consumption. Additionally, the purity of hydration is critical. Electrolytes, including sodium, potassium, and magnesium, are of paramount importance in preserving the hydrostatic equilibrium within and around cells, including the cerebral region. Electrolyte balance is a factor in promoting optimal neural function.

To promote cognitive health, it is advisable for individuals to proactively implement hydration strategies. This entails ensuring a steady and adequate consumption of water throughout the day. Incorporating fruit and vegetable consumption, which are abundant in water, can additionally promote proper hydration. Furthermore, it is critical to consider environmental variables, including temperature and humidity, as they have the potential to elevate the body's demand for fluids.

The Importance Of Social Relationships To Cognitive Health

In addition to cognitive supplements and exercises, it is impossible to exaggerate the importance of social connections to cognitive health. Human beings are by nature social beings, and the caliber of social interactions significantly influences cognitive function and mental health.

Social Engagement and Cognitive Stimulation: Cognitive stimulation is achieved through the facilitation of social connections, participation in group activities, and engagement in meaningful conversations. Social interactions demand cognitive processing of information, interpretation of social signals, and navigation of intricate social dynamics. Engaging in these activities may potentially enhance cognitive reserve and aid in the preservation of cognitive abilities.

Evidence supports the notion that strong social connections may contribute to a decelerated rate of cognitive decline in older individuals. Social engagement is thought to offer a safeguarding influence, potentially alleviating the consequences of cognitive alterations associated with aging. Consistent participation in social gatherings, including team sports, literary societies, and community events, provides prospects for intellectual and interpersonal growth.

Emotional support and cognitive resilience are closely intertwined, with social connections serving as vital contributors to emotional well-being. Individuals can prevent the detrimental effects of stress, anxiety, and other emotional challenges on their cognitive function by receiving emotional support from family and friends.

On the contrary, there exists a correlation between social isolation and loneliness, and cognitive deterioration, as well as an elevated susceptibility to ailments like dementia. Insufficient regular social interactions impede cognitive function by depriving the brain of necessary stimulation. Therefore, upholding robust social connections is not solely advantageous for psychological well-being, but also crucial for the preservation of cognitive capabilities.

CHAPTER FIVE

A Holistic Approach To Cognitive Health Concludes.

To achieve optimal cognitive functioning, it is crucial to embrace a comprehensive strategy that incorporates cognitive enhancement, nootropics, adequate hydration, and social interactions.

By incorporating cognitive exercises that stimulate the mind, nootropics that may offer supplementary cognitive support, maintaining adequate hydration to guarantee optimal brain function, and nurturing emotional well-being through social connections, a holistic approach to cognitive health is fostered. The incorporation of these components into one's daily routine may aid in the preservation of cognitive functions and the promotion of mental health across the entire lifespan.

Investigating Alternative Approaches To Achieve Mental Clarity

To commence the pursuit of mental clarity, one must initially adopt alternative therapies that surpass traditional practices.

Acupuncture, yoga, aromatherapy, and mindfulness meditation are a few examples of alternative practices that are gaining in popularity.

Mindfulness meditation, which has its origins in ancient contemplative traditions, promotes the cultivation of awareness and clarity of thought by encouraging individuals to concentrate on the present moment. Yoga, by its integration of bodily postures and regulation of respiration, not only augments flexibility but also fosters psychological tranquility.

Aromatherapy utilizes the capacity of fragrances to affect one's disposition and emotions. Lavender, chamomile, and eucalyptus essential oils are renowned for their contemplative qualities, which contribute to the alleviation of tension and the revitalization of the mind. It is believed that acupuncture, an ancient Chinese technique involving the insertion of thin needles into specific locations on the body, can restore energy balance and improve mental and emotional health.

Alternative therapies offer individuals a wide range of

resources to investigate, enabling them to ascertain which practices align most closely with their specific requirements and inclinations.

Executing Lifestyle Modifications To Achieve Durable Outcomes

Although alternative therapies may provide transient solace and newfound understanding, the adoption of healthier lifestyle habits is essential for attaining enduring outcomes in the quest for mental lucidity. A critical element entails attending to the fundamental pillars of psychological wellness, namely sleep, nutrition, and physical activity.

The sleep of sufficient quantity and quality is fundamental for mental clarity. The implementation of a regular sleep schedule, the creation of an environment that is conducive to sleep, and the reduction of screen usage before bedtime are all crucial practices.

In addition, nutrition is critical, as a well-balanced diet supplies the brain with the essential nutrients required for its maximum efficiency. The consumption of whole foods, antioxidants, and omega-3 fatty acids has the potential to enhance mental resilience.

Engaging in physical activity can significantly enhance one's cognitive acuity. Endorphins are released during exercise, stress hormones are decreased, and cognitive function is improved.

A sustainable and pleasurable regimen can be established by discovering a form of exercise that corresponds with an individual's preferences, be it leisurely walks, yoga sessions, or more rigorous activities.

In addition to attending to fundamental concerns, it is critical to accurately recognize and efficiently handle stressors. This may entail establishing limits, developing effective time management skills, or consulting with a professional for assistance.

Promoting positive interpersonal relationships and establishing social bonds are additional substantial contributors to mental health, as they facilitate emotional solace and nurture a feeling of inclusion.

CHAPTER SIX

Monitoring Development And Modifying Approaches

As one commences the pursuit of mental clarity, monitoring one's progress and maintaining a willingness to modify strategies emerge as indispensable elements of the voyage.

The utilization of mental health applications or the maintenance of a journal can assist in the monitoring of energy levels, mood swings, and the efficacy of various therapeutic practices.

Consistent reflection enables individuals to discern patterns and triggers that exert either a positive or negative influence on mental clarity. One might observe, for instance, that mindfulness meditation is notably efficacious during periods of heightened work-related tension, whereas moments of anxiety are more effectively alleviated through yoga.

By comprehending these patterns, individuals are empowered to customize their approach according to various circumstances, thereby maximizing the efficacy of their selected therapies.

Furthermore, consulting with experts in the field can provide invaluable perspectives and individualized approaches. Mental health practitioners, such as counselors, therapists, and holistic practitioners, are capable of offering assistance in managing obstacles and honing an individual's strategy toward psychological wellness.

The refinement of lifestyle modifications and alternative therapies is guided by a comprehensive comprehension of individual requirements attained through collaboration with healthcare providers.

Conclusion

Exploring alternative therapies, incorporating lifestyle modifications, and consistently monitoring progress constitute an interconnected and ever-evolving process in the quest for mental clarity.

The expedition necessitates an individual's dedication to self-exploration, as they engage in diverse experimental endeavors in pursuit of that which personally resonates with them.

Alternative therapies, which draw inspiration from both historical practices and modern perspectives, present a wide range of opportunities for individuals to investigate and incorporate into their everyday routines. A variety of disciplines, including aromatherapy and mindfulness meditation, offer both immediate and long-term benefits for mental resilience.

The establishment of enduring improvements in mental lucidity is predicated on the adoption of habitual modifications.

By making sleep, nutrition, physical activity, and stress management a priority, people establish the groundwork for long-term wellness. Making adjustments to one's lifestyle necessitates commitment and regularity, enabling individuals to confront the intricacies of contemporary existence with enhanced fortitude.

Constant monitoring of progress and strategic adjustments guarantees that the endeavor to attain mental clarity sustains its adaptability and responsiveness. Developing a more profound comprehension of personal requirements through the use of journaling, reflection, and professional consultation enables the enhancement and optimization of therapeutic methodologies.

In summary, the investigation of alternative therapeutic modalities and the adoption of lifestyle modifications provide a comprehensive and individualized strategy for attaining mental lucidity. By adopting these strategies and maintaining a heightened awareness of personal requirements, people can cultivate a mental state that is both resilient and lucid, capable of withstanding the rigors of the contemporary world.